YOUR
TALKING
CAT

Jack Richter

Your Talking Cat
Jack Richter

Copyright © MMVI The Windsor Group

Published MMVI by The Windsor Group,
The Old School House,
1 St John's Court,
Moulsham Street,
Chelmsford,
Essex CM2 0LD

Typeset by SJ Design and Publishing, Bromley, Kent

ISBN 1-903904-60-9

Contents

With Thanks...

To my Grandma Elsa, gone to her reward, who never turned away any of the little cats I brought to her without first giving each one a piece of liver or chicken, or a saucer of milk, plus some kind words . . .

To friends with cats whose personal experiences with their intelligent, responsive pets helped give background and depth to this book . . .

To Rosalie, a special friend, who has five cats and who selflessly contributed so many hours to the preparation and writing of this book. Her exceptional talents are evident in several of the 'Purr-sonals', as well as in her 'Cat Bye-Laws' article . . .

To Anna Mae, who gave me valuable editorial judgements and research support from Day One of my writing this book . . .

To 'Trax', my little buddy and favourite cat, who lives across from the railway station. He just looked at me and I knew I had to write YOUR TALKING CAT . . .

Foreword

Occasionally, I stop at a little coffee shop and newspaper stand near the railway station. Sitting outside that store on nice days, enjoying the morning sun, is a handsome little grey cat I've nicknamed 'Trax'.

'Trax' is a male cat, about a year old, who serves the store as a mouse-chaser. He has very light green eyes that can almost hypnotise you if you look into them for more than fifteen or twenty seconds. In his eyes, you can almost turn back time to when his furry ancestors, thousands of years ago, lived in a completely uncivilised world.

'Trax' has eyes that somehow make you feel that he knows more than you do, that by only studying you for a moment or two, he could almost foretell your future.

Maybe it's because he looks so serene and

silent as he watches the morning commuters race for their trains into the city. Maybe it's because all those depressing headlines in the morning papers never concern him, and nothing disturbs his natural euphoria, his obvious, enviable joie de vivre.

In fact, I think it was 'Trax' who sent me to my typewriter to start writing this book about cats. It was 'Trax' who suddenly made me realise that a cat can be the almost perfect 'antidote to civilisation'. Without so much as a "meow" in response to my greeting, 'Trax' communicated something to me that slowed me down to a walk and made me think. I had been putting off the writing of a book like this, but one look from 'Trax' got me going. Who says cats don't communicate? He, or she, never met 'Trax'.

Prologue

Why a theatrical word instead of a book word, like 'Introduction?' Because from what I've seen, 'theatre' describes a cat's communications in most of its aspects.

Because, as the remarkable musical *Cats* underscored, cats are basically creatures of strong emotion, changeable and often moody. These, too, are the makings of great theatre.

People share much of the same sensitivity and many of the same emotions as cats experience, which adds to the dramatic (theatre) effect of personifying cats in human form.

In general, people try to mask their innate theatrics. Cats revel in them. And in their own unique language, cats use showmanship much more effectively than most people. Since they are 'uncivilised' free spirits, they abandon themselves to the mood or emotion of the moment, while people, for fear of creating a wrong image, frequently sublimate their feelings.

Maybe a cat's obsession with theatrics in talking is one reason why most cats in their natural environment live out their lives without ulcers, high blood pressure and arteriosclerosis. And, maybe, when they try living in a human environment, imitating the attitudes and life-styles of their people, it accounts for so many millions of neurotic cats; prone to those same human ills.

Back to theatre. What I discovered, or re-discovered, in writing this book is that anyone who is seriously interested in a Talking Cat had better first know that a cat is probably *Mother Nature's foremost exponent of 'show me' language, i.e., a language of both visual and auditory components.* A cat never just talks. She carefully programmes each thought in her mind and then expounds her ideas, surrounding them with flourishes and staging wild histrionics, and even 'voice-music' backgrounds that turn a simple request to 'go out' into a mini-musical play. If at first you don't understand her, you always get a good show.

When you watch a cat, you are watching the embodiment of a natural writer, a gifted actor and singer, a director and a producer – all in one kinetic package!

As a lucky cat-owner, you have been given a lifetime, front-row-centre seat to see and hear little dramas and musicals of real theatrical quality. Her vocabulary and phonetics, along with orchestrated body movements and vocalising to match, reflect the theatre on Broadway in New York and the West End in London every time.

It is essential that you *concentrate*, as you would in a theatre, with your eyes, your ears and your emotions, or you may miss something and lose the message.

Remarkably, a cat's vocalising, which is purely emotion-in-sound, changes with each mood being enacted. It follows the pattern of traditional opera or musicals, using dulcet, low-volume, relaxing tones and rhythms when the subject is loving and friendly, and swings into brassy and abrasive sounds when something frightening or unfriendly enters the stage.

Each cat is endowed with his or her own

pattern of communicating. Some cats talk a lot; others do very little talking because, like some people who are naturally gregarious or naturally withdrawn, the degree of communication varies.

On a scale of 1 to 10, a particular cat may rate a '3' on a 'like-to-talk' question. Another, an aggressive Tom, may be a '9' on the same scale.

But that's purr-sonality. Yet, every cat born into the kingdom of cats is a communicator who chooses to use the skills when, where and how it suits her or him. In fact, a cat with more innate communications skills may use those skills less than half as much as a less-intelligent cat with almost total extrovert characteristics.

What is even more important, some cats use their voices to coordinate messages with body language; some rarely use their voices and rely instead on brilliant gestures and fast footwork to make known their wishes and needs.

How much 'Body Language' do some cats use in putting across their messages? Again, it varies. But body language is so natural for a lithe and healthy cat that 90% or more of understanding what a cat is telling you emanates from her almost unbelievable abilities as a mime, matching those of the great Marcel Marceau of Paris.

Mostly, the meows you hear are used for making the message more interesting, more urgent or just more dramatic. At best, the Talking Cat will make maximum use of both visual and auditory talents, but the ultimate reading of an intelligent cat's script, written and directed by the cat herself, depends upon the visual image she projects. More on that special subject a bit later in the book.

It will make your cat language-learning course an enjoyable breeze when you think of your cat as a kind of su-purr-star in her own world, always at home on stage, always ready to 'go on' for you. All it takes is a little invitation from you!

Your kitten's talking to you, Miss.
Seems to want a hug and a kiss!

Your kitten's talking to you, Sir.
Don't you hear that quiet purr?

Chapter I
The Great CommuniCats

CAN A CAT TALK?

Definitely YES, but in a language that requires just a little determination and a little spare time to master.

For the purpose of this book, we will refer to it simply as CAT LANGUAGE.

Joan Bernstein, whose brilliant work is presented in the following chapter, is an outstanding authority about the breeding and behaviour of cats. When I asked her to comment about cats and their 'conversations', she volunteered the following:

"Cats, like people, may be very different in the degree to which they like to communicate or remain silent. One cat will `talk' almost all the time; another will limit the use of her voice to simple requests for her needs or to be let out."

Perhaps your cat is a real 'talker' and will

respond at almost any time to your invitation to join her in a talk session. Perhaps she leads a less-talkative life, disdaining delivery of most vocal messages to people.

Either way, the *body language* aspect of Cat Language is probably more revealing to the average person than the 'background music' of the cat's voice language.

A cat is a master of the art of pantomime and relies heavily on its face and body 'signals' to tell you what it wants, or how it feels.

CAT CONVERSATION

Every authority on the subject of conversations with cats agrees on the fact *that they have an intelligent form of language, with an established set of ritualistic symbols and body movements, combined with musically-discordant but rhythmically-balanced vocal chords.*

Could those same vocal chords pick up on the phonetic sounds of another language, like English? No one knows, nor has any known research been done in this area of study that indicates the possibility of a scientific breakthrough. Hopefully, researchers will find the subject challenging enough to open up this avenue of study, in the same way that the famous Moog Synthesiser opened up the field of creative musical sounds.

First among the landmark researchers of his time was the famous English naturalist Charles Robert Darwin, who made scientific history with his writing of 'The Origin of Species by Natural Selection'.

In his 'Expressions of Emotions', he states: 'Cats use their voices as a means of expression and utter, under various emotions and desires, at least six or seven different sounds.'

Darwin's findings were correct, as proved repeatedly by later proponents of his work, who have isolated as many as 100 variations on the voices of cats, *but fixed on 20 which are audible to the human ear*. No one can ever question the fact that cats do talk rapidly among themselves, slower with people.

Later, a stream of writers and researchers, including Champfleury, and Abbe Galiani, through the works of Carl Van Vechten ('Tiger in the House'), contributed to a continuing study of cat communications. Their unique language is becoming a higher priority subject with each passing year.

CONCLUSION: DOES A CAT TALK?

Half, or more, of the cat's communication is a silent language, spoken with its very versatile and responsive body parts.

Along with these motions and gestures, Your Talking Cat orchestrates various sounds, somewhat like a smart dolphin, to complete each message.

You owe it to your cat (and to yourself) to start communicating more effectively and more often. If you don't, you'll never know what fun you've been missing.

F

P

D

Chapter II
The CommuniCat Purr-sonality

If you're a keen observer of cats, you know that:

A CAT cannot just tell you something and let it go at that. She dramatises it, repeats it, toys with it, embellishes it. A cat is a supurrb actor.

A CAT never just 'talks'. She does some vocalising, yes. But she wants you to notice her eyes, her ears, her body language and, especially, her always-moving tail. If you miss her words, at least you get a great show!

A CAT makes up her mind, after studying you, as to whether or not you are worth talking to. If not, she can turn and go to sleep on the spot, ignoring you completely.

A CAT knows the art of communicating by nature. She uses two speaker's codes to say something – the audible code and the visible code. When she makes a strong statement, all of her becomes involved.

A CAT lets you know if you're her cup of tea or not. If she cannot be sure of you, or something you are carrying, or someone you brought home, she may swing her tail rather violently to allay her indecision. But once the tail action stops, you'll have her decision.

A CAT looks upon you and the whole world as if everything in sight is part of her territory and is possessed by her. Notice in her walk and in her 'watching time' sessions how brazenly she tells you that.

A CAT likes her comforts and peace of mind above all, and if you disturb those patterns, you immediately enter the 'trouble' corner of her mind. She has a style of communicating her displeasure in her face, as well as her behaviour towards you.

A CAT chooses her sound vocabulary very carefully. If she does not make her point the first time she speaks, she will repeat the same sounds again and again, but much louder, until you pay attention to her. She stays right on the point and is never distracted from the target.

A CAT communicates in somewhat the same

way that she sets out on a hunting expedition. She sets up her objective, observes her prey, or her prey's habitat, for as long as it takes to catch her quarry unawares. Then, she strikes with almost lightning speed. In her communications, she follows the same, observe-and-wait tactic, choosing just the right moment to approach you with her request.

A CAT is the kind of communicator from whom everyone could take lessons.

A CAT makes the pastime of watching a cat more than just 'interesting'. It makes it *profitable*, if you can only apply the lessons you learn in this book.

A CAT is astute enough to recognise small differences in sounds that relate to her comfort or pleasure. She can distinguish the sound of one car engine from another, and know when the man or lady of the house is arriving.

A CAT associates the different sounds from the kitchen – the whirring of the tin-opener, dishes being arranged at the table, glasses being taken from the cabinet – as the rituals that happily accompany mealtimes.

A CAT lives for the moments that tell her that her food is being dished out, and she is there watching before you've scooped out the last spoonful. A cat's communicating ability is probably at its highest level of activity around mealtime.

Chapter III
Supercat People-Helpers

AN EXCLUSIVE INTERVIEW WITH JOAN BERNSTEIN, A FELINE-FACILITATED THERAPIST

Joan Bernstein is a feline-facilitated therapist, which is her definition of a person who implements therapeutic techniques by using cats as intermediaries between practitioner and client.

In Bernstein's case, the cats are her 'terrific Tonkinese', a Siamese-Burmese hybrid breed uniquely suited to this work by temperament and wrapping (their mink-like coats seem to be hypo-allergenic).

Stable personalities range from normal to psychotic, in environments ranging from conventionally domestic to locked psychiatric wards.

Among the average clients, however, are

many whose immune systems have been impaired by age and/or illness. Fortunately, these clients usually can enjoy the company of a Tonkinese without the threat of an allergic reaction.

Bernstein is a long-time cat-breeder whose Shotoku Cattery is respected throughout the cat-fanciers' world. She has bred Siamese, Colorpoint Shorthairs, Burmese and Oriental Shorthairs. But her beloved Tonkinese are a composite of her two favourite early breeds, the Siamese and Burmese.

Superbly intelligent, humorous and gregarious, the Tonkinese, Bernstein feels, have a natural inclination for therapy work. The rest is up to the breeder, who must capitalise on the basics to raise cats capable of performing as co-therapists.

Not every cat – even among Tonks – is right for the job. The cats Bernstein uses for her 'Have Cats, Will Travel/Cat Assisted Therapy Service' are bonded to humans from birth.

As kittens, they are helped to accept a broad spectrum of environmental disturbances and situations. They may begin going to nursing homes with Bernstein and their experienced parents, aunts, uncles, cousins, etc., at about three months of age.

This is actually their first 'test'. Those that 'pass' eventually grow into the routine and become certified therapy cats. Among the best are Bernstein's Cat Fanciers' Association Grand Champion Shotoku Chutzpurr; Grand Champion Shotoku Fame; Grand Premier Shotoku Gwyndav, and several Champions who are 'working on' Grand status.

Why? Because these are cats that have learned to tolerate noisy, crowded show halls; handling by many strangers, such as cat show judges; travel by car and plane; strange hotel rooms, and smells, sounds, sights and activity that rarely happen to the average domestic cat.

These cats usually are those who also have a sense of presence and a love of stage drama; otherwise, they wouldn't be successful show cats. And it is really this special essence that makes the best therapy cats.

Bernstein says her cats are the "bridge" between the client and the practitioner. They set up "the lines of communication that may make it possible, eventually, to reach a person who is otherwise unreachable."

She is referring to clients who may have disorders which cause withdrawal, severe depression, catatonia, coma, or voluntary or involuntary rejection of human intervention.

"Cats don't need nouns, verbs and grammar to communicate", Bernstein says. "They may use sounds that combine vowels and consonants in patterns that humans who are 'tuned in' can interpret – but they don't have to.

Like actors, especially mimes, they are acutely sensitive to, and adept at, body language.

But above all, cats communicate telepathically. That's the only word I know to define their communication skills. I've watched it happen – and been lucky enough to participate – too often to try to deny it. It's an extra-sensory ability that occurs as naturally in cats as the ability to speak does in humans."

AUTHOR'S COMMENTS: That statement, in a direct interview which she is aware may reach several hundred thousands of readers, made a deep impression on me. This gracious lady, who was featured in a PBS network television documentary created by the prestigious National Geographic magazine and entitled 'Cat: Caressing the Tiger', convinced me that my conclusions about cats were on target.

As one of the world's leading authorities on cat communications, as a state-of-the-art practitioner of this highly-specialised service, using specially-adapted cats, and as a foremost breeder of exotic cats for many years, her words have the unmistakeable ring of solid gold. What she does not know about cats is miniscule, indeed.

Until that moment, I had not discussed this thought with many of my intellectual friends whom I thought would consider me something of a dreamer.

However, I steadfastly held on to the feeling that from conversations with friends who have cats, from a file full of background information, and from my own experience with certain cats, this almost alarming phenomenon unique to cats – the power to communicate by means beyond the five senses – actually exists! Thus, my interview with Joan Bernstein took on an even more exciting personal dimension.

A group of autistic youngsters are among the clients who may refuse to interact with other people, yet are unusually responsive to cats. One electively mute youth loves to stroke their fur and is fascinated by their movements. He especially likes his favourite cat, 'Moth', to rub her head under his chin, purr and 'talk' to him. When Bernstein first approached him with 'Moth', he would sign 'cat'. An early indication that he might attempt speech with the cat as a catalyst occurred when Bernstein showed him how to mimic the cat's purr, and the youth laughingly complied.

In the 13th month of therapy, Bernstein placed 'Moth' on his lap and signed, then verbalised "cat", as usual. The youngster grinned, and with a gleeful glint in his eye, sighed and pronounced "cat", as if he'd been doing it every day of his life. Since then, all of his counsellors are helping him develop a working vocabulary, but 'cat' is still his favourite word.

Bernstein uses the cats to help clients stimulate and exercise damaged limbs, damaged senses and disabled mental or emotional processes. Years of related and unrelated experience and education have contributed to her skill, but she says the most vital aspect of her work is 'reading' her cats and following through. It is no longer a conscious process, she says.

"When you're really concentrating, you can almost feel the electricity, the air hums with tension, like an electromagnetic field", Bernstein says. "It's astonishing what can happen then. That's when you're most likely to get a breakthrough. Of course, it doesn't always happen. It's hard work, and sometimes the cats just want to play! There's nothing wrong with that, either. Learning to totally relax like a cat is healthy, too."

Bernstein works with clients in a variety of health-care and health-related facilities in Long Island, NY. While there are numerous groups which provide animal-assisted therapy, using dogs and horses, in particular, at this time Bernstein's is the only professional programme designed to bring cats to clients.

Not to be confused with volunteer visiting pet programmes, "which contribute greatly to the quality of life, especially in institutional settings", Bernstein sees her work as a "proven, viable alternative to conventional therapies, a springboard that can open channels for all the professionals on a client's team to develop new approaches to old problems."

It was late evening when I left Joan Bernstein,

having driven some 60 miles to meet her, and ready to return another 60 miles. But even if the mileage had been double that, what she had to say in the interview was worth many times any inconvenience I may have had in reaching her. I should like very much to be her friend.

R

Z

Chapter IV
Tracking the CommuniCats

THE CAT AS A SACRED SYMBOL

Egyptian mythology placed the Goddess Bast high in the hierarchy of the gods. She represents the good side of fire and the bearer of good fortune for households which paid homage to her. Her sister, and rival, represented the malevolent deity, the raging part of fire, the bearer of bad fortune.

While in earliest mythology Bast had the head of a lioness and the body of a woman, she was depicted in sculptured figures as a seated cat during the 26th Egyptian Dynasty. In one of the statues, she has a vase in her hand which has the name of the goddess written in hieroglyphics. It signifies the pouring of oil or water upon her worshippers, which was frequently the theme of religious symbolism in ensuing religious history.

Since the cat was the favoured symbol of Bast, several of them have been unearthed as mummies throughout the region surrounding the shrine at Bubastis, the largest and most important sacred city of ancient Egypt. This city became the centre of an annual festival called Bubasteia. Egyptians from distant cities and towns would flock to Bubastis, which represented the modern-day Rome or Mecca, surrounded by musicians and drinking wine as they went. Most travelled by water in large barges and one report by the ancient Greek historian Herodotus estimated that some 700,000 people would arrive each year in a holiday atmosphere similar to the later Roman dedication to Bacchus, the God of Wine.

Herodotus gathered the first known chronological facts about the events that led to the capture of Bubastis and its destruction by the Persians under Memnon several hundred years B.C. A coin was minted later in Egypt that paid homage to the almost forgotten cat-worshipping city, which shows the goddess holding what appears to be a cat in her lap.

The colourful accounts of Bubastis, written by the versatile Herodotus, along with his historical reports of many cities of the Near East, earned him the title of the 'Father of History'. Even today, his carefully-dated writings about the conquests by Persia of several parts of Egypt make fascinating reading. In later periods of history, people throughout Europe read Herodotus' detailed commentaries on the cat goddess and her remarkable little felines.

In ancient Egypt, anyone found mistreating or killing a cat was summarily executed! It's no wonder, then, that wealthy Egyptians, who probably studied cats and observed them in all of their nocturnal festivities, came to the conclusion that behind their enigmatic eyes was a world beyond this world, not given to mortals to understand.

To put them in a category with gods was just the next logical step. Because, weren't gods totally mysterious, totally beyond our human ken, like cats?

If a cat can communicate itself into becoming a minor god, I would say that she fully deserves the title 'communicator'.

Incidentally, could it be that both Napoleon Bonaparte and Adolf Hitler, who despised cats and would not permit a cat in their presence, could not stand the competition? Or could it be that when they looked into a cat's face, they felt that this arrogant little creature was actually reading their twisted minds? It's an interesting conjecture.

In our times, the cat has succeeded in developing entire industries around the species. They include publishing empires, packaged food manufacturing giants, product distribution systems, and the like, with thousands of people in their employ.

By all means, cats are great communicators and this book salutes their ability to make people understand almost everything they want or desire. Then, to motivate people to go out and *get* the things they want, their communicating art reaches the apex of achievement.

EARLY COMMUNICATION WITH CATS

In one of the most widely-circulated books of the 18th century, *Histoire Naturelle*, by French nobleman Comte Georges Louis LeClerc de

Buffon (a member of several Royal Academies of Europe), the naturalist gives his description of cats and their personalities and concludes: "Cats, while animals of prey, are useful as domestics; that while showing wisdom, they have more attachments to places than to people; they have light, adroit, clean and voluptuous bodies; they love ease and search out the softest furniture; they take naps all day long and so repose and rest themselves; they are pretty as young cats and possess a very proper way to amuse children (if the strokes of their paws were not to be feared); they seem to have a natural dread of water, cold and bad smells; they are attracted to perfumes and allow themselves to be caressed by peoplewho wear them, and they have eyes that 'imbibe light' in day and give off light at night."

His last notion was incorrect, since cat's eyes merely reflect light, as they do when car headlights beam into them. Since his time, many important writers have referred to cats, each with somewhat dissimilar views, demonstrating that cats can say different things to different people at different times.

It was some time in the distant past that man,

with no more knowledge of how to share his thoughts with other men than any other animal, decided that he should begin to organise the sounds of his voice into a form that we now call language.

He was intelligent enough to see that certain of his needs, such as hunting or fishing for food, protecting himself and his family from wild animals at night while asleep, and finding the safest place to raise his children, all required some form of *communication* with his fellow tribesmen.

Up to that time, like the tiger, the lion, the gorilla or the chimpanzee, it had been enough to utter a series of grunts, along with appropriate body language and grimaces, to let others know his moods or desires. But, because man had a brain much larger, much more adaptable and more ingenious than his four-footed companions, he began to separate himself from their life-style. He began to invent visual symbols to represent ideas, even began to measure time in illustrated calendars on his cave wall.

The rest of the story we all know. Man has developed and refined his life and environment until he has overcome most of his pre-historic problems but one – himself. (He will have accomplished that, once he eliminates wars, famine, pollution, etc.).

In reaching down to his 'little brother', the cat, who is willing to share civilised life with man, we have taken a giant step in the direction of helping another species achieve, through better communication, some of the advantages and pleasures which civilisation can provide.

When you strive to build a better 'language bridge' to your cat, an animal with great pride and equally great ability to learn, you have stepped back into the dim past. You are helping a very interesting survivor of time, like man, himself, to step another few feet out of the dark jungles and into the light of useful knowledge.

Will education in language confuse a cat? Will your cat swing her tail back and forth or in a straight line to demonstrate her feeling of being insecure?

Looking at it from a cat's point of view, it's easy to see why some of our actions and decisions might generate some moments of confusion and wonderment. Why, she will ponder, all this new attention to her body language and meows?

Which brings us to the central objective of this book: to arrange to surprise her with a little more fond attention, a little more willingness to let her 'strut her stuff' in front of you and members of the family, for whom she has affection. More important, she will be playing her favourite character – herself!

Next to digging into a fresh dish of expensive fish or dating her favourite Tom, Your Talking Cat loves being on stage. So, 'make her day'!

O

M

Chapter V

Thinking Cat Language

TALKING CAT: READ THE WORDS & MUSIC TOGETHER

Just as any message of a vocalised song combines the lyrics (words) with a sound background (music), every time you converse with your cat, the message is being presented in a words-and-music package.

All great actors and actresses use these same visual-plus-vocal effects to provide their audiences with exciting eye-and-ear reception of the author's concepts. When they play dramatic roles in one of the great operas, a *third* dimension of staging is added – they use body language, words *and* music, orchestrated by first-class musicians, to focus total attention and interest upon what is being said by the writers.

Your Talking Cat is doing the same kind of

orchestration every time it approaches you to speak. The director and conductor of the staging is the cat's lively and intelligent brain. The brain directs the muscular actions of the eyes, the ears, the body and tail, and it tells the cat's vocal chords exactly how and when to release the sounds that accompany the signals. Science is only beginning to comprehend these multi-level words-and-music messages, which every cat is born to use. It is only that limited human hearing and concentration may permit more of these sophisticated cat-language messages to pass unheeded and unanswered. Your Talking Cat changes all that.

TALKING CAT: THE FIRST LANGUAGE BRIDGE

At the United Nations, where people of many languages meet to master-plan world harmony, language and thought projection become critically important every day. But language has yet to become universal, and a delegate with a vital topic on his agenda, delivered in his native tongue, may be understood only by a small group of the membership.

Without interpreters, equipped with state-of-the-art microphones and receivers, there could be no speeches. It would be the United Nations' Tower of Babel. The first person to invent an electronic language that would permit five delegates from five countries speaking different languages to speak directly to each other without interpreters to alter meanings would certainly win a Nobel Prize!

The same challenge faces the communications experts in merging Cat Language with English. At this time, the most we can accomplish is that YOU, with command of English, will act as an interpreter. If a deaf-and-dumb person can speak in sign language, a blind person can read with Braille, then you can learn to decode messages from your cat every day and intelligently. Try it and see, after you get deeper into this book. It works, thanks to the introduction of YOUR TALKING CAT.

ALL ABOUT CAT MOODS AND CAT SOUNDS

Musicologists would appreciate the innate ability of a cat to adapt the principles of creating musical sounds and compositions. The basics of any melody, pitch and rhythm are demonstrated every time a cat speaks. Together, they deliver the cat composer's message.

When a cat talks to you, the music of her message is there, either purring in rhythm, or meowing in rhythm. Maybe you never quite paid attention before, but at your next opportunity *listen*. You will hear a message spoken while you *see and feel the message spoken* at the same time!

What takes years of study for someone to learn in the entertainment field, a cat will offer you quickly, at nor charge, and very willingly. If 'show business' interests you. Your Talking Cat will fascinate you with the dramatic abilities and musical talents that she embodies.

At times when her life is filled with discord, doubt, fear, jealousy or conflict, she plays out and sings out a matching discordant role. When it's time for harmony and loving relationships, the entire scene changes and she lets you share in her happy mood. She leaves nothing unsaid.

Cat Language becomes easy to understand and enjoyable to translate when you approach the learning process with a firm appreciation of the fact that cats are always acting out or talking out a feeling, just as an actor does on stage. And your little theatrical star makes the finest teacher you could find, anywhere.

U

V

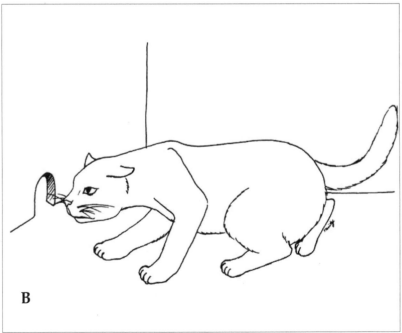

B

Chapter VI
Primer of Cat Language

THE FOUR STEPS TO OPEN THE DOOR SYSTEM

This book simplifies the learning of Cat Language. In four basic steps, anyone who wants to communicate with a cat can become fluent with the language in the time it takes to read the Sunday newspaper from cover-to-cover.

The first step in learning any language is to memorise its basic code – the alphabet. The 26-letter English alphabet has letters from A to Z – each with a phonetic sound, each capable of enough variations of use that, together, the 26 letters can create thousands of words!

The first step in learning Cat Language is to memorise the face, body and tail symbols (signals) that spell out the cat's messages in different combinations. **Each message is**

played out like a game of charades in which you, the audience, are deciphering the meanings, while Your Talking Cat is acting out the clues!

Each time you get into conversation with Your Talking Cat, you will become a little more adept at figuring out the charade message until, eventually, you will be decoding her mind in no time at all. Again, the learning of a worthwhile skill takes practice, practice, practice.

Memorise the picture/alphabet of your cat's body signals, start memorising a mental change of meows, and you're on your way to language proficiency.

The key words to open the door are:
1. **MEMORISE**
2. **OBSERVE**
3. **INTERPRET**
4. **PRACTISE**

1. MEMORISE

The primer of the Cat Language Chart on the `next two pages suggests in visuals the kinds of communication signals that Your Talking Cat uses to convey her thoughts to you. Actually, they total less than the number of different 'meows' that a cat uses to 'underscore' and to reinforce the precise meaning of what she is saying, both vocally and visually.

In less time than it takes to read the next 20 pages or so of this book, your eye will train itself to watch for all these signals. You'll flash back to them in cat talk. Then, practice alone will imprint this alphabet of signs into your memory.

IMPORTANT: Cat behaviour experts will admit that no set strict guidelines about cat behaviour applies to every cat in every situation. Therefore, remember that they are only 'guides' and may not show exactly what your cat is saying. A horizontal tail may say "I'm here to talk to you" or be part of her signal to "Let me out!" Your personal experience, repeatedly talking to Your Talking Cat, will provide the answers.

2. OBSERVE

A talking cat spends more than half of its waking hours in the act of **observing**. It is the primary reason why a cat knows exactly when and where to approach her master or mistress. She has spent many hours, usually at a distance or almost out of sight, watching when her mistress, for example, a young mother completes each of her daily chores and is ready to pay attention to **her**, the cat. She will watch through the getting of the children to the school bus, often accompanying the children to the corner and returning, then the breakfast clean-up, then the getting ready to shop and waiting for her mistress to return with groceries, which she checks out quietly to see if **her** food is included. Then the telephoning, always a boring time listening to jabber which the cat does not understand. Then a moment of calm in the storm when the young woman can turn to her and say: "Now it's you and I, Tabby! What is on your mind?" She watches, watches, watches. This is a cat's gift to her owner.

This book suggests that it now becomes your interesting responsibility, as a Cat Language enthusiast, to pay her the same kind of compliment – let her know that you are watching HER for a few 'quality moments' through the day.

3. INTERPRET

When you become expert in any subject, the

CAT LANGUAGE

STATE OF BEING:	FACIAL EXPRESSION POSITION OF EYES AND EARS	
HAPPY		EYES: NARROWED AND BLINKING EARS: UPRIGHT AND ALERT
CURIOUS		EYES: WIDE OPEN AND FIXATED EARS: UPRIGHT
DEFENSIVE (THREATENED)		EYES: PUPILS DILATED EARS: DOWNWARD
ANNOYED		EYES: EYELIDS LOWERED, PUPILS DILATED EARS: SLIGHTLY DOWNWARD
ANGRY		EYES: WIDE AND DILATED EARS: FLATTENED AND PULLED BACK

CHART

SOUNDS EMITTED	TAIL POSITION / ACTION	
PURR, PURR FOR A FAVOURED PERSON		STRAIGHT UP
INQUISITIVE PURRS		RAISED AND CURVED
HISSING AND SNARLING		BRISTLED AND ARCHED
LOW, THROATY RUMBLING		TWITCHING OR SWINGING DEPENDING ON DEGREE OF AGITATION
HISSING AND GROWLING		BUSHY AND LOWERED

skills you have acquired help you know from experience how to handle a situation in the right way. This applies to skills like carpentry, sketching, writing, piano-playing, etc.

Your expertise in Cat Language will develop rapidly. As you devote more time to memorising the alphabet of signals and then in observing (which suggest analysing, too) what your cat is telling you.

After keen observation and application of your purrsonal knowledge of the different ways your cat reacts to different situations, your interpretations will get more and more accurate.

4. PRACTISE

'Practice', on a piano or any skill, 'makes perfect', as you know. On the following pages of this book, you'll have a 'purr-fect' opportunity to test your memory of the Body and Face Language cats use to tell you what they're thinking.

A. BODY MOVES

To express her many and various emotions, your cat responds in much the same way as a human being. She feels nervousness, boredom, affection, curiosity, happiness and unhappiness.

She gets jealous, feels inferior, gets angry or annoyed. Each of these 'ATTITUDES' is expressed by a special kind of voice and/or body language signal. It will be useful to know these terms:

HEAD 'ATTITUDE'

A cat will nuzzle you or butt you with its head to show affection or to get your attention.

EAR 'ATTITUDE'

Alert and high, your cat is ready to listen and join in the conversation. When ears are flat or lying at the sides, your cat is not quite sure of what is happening. Ears that are low and close to the head warn: "Don't take another step toward me!" When ears are in a downward position, the cat is expressing wariness. "Let me think about this", she is saying.

TAIL 'ATTITUDE'

A tail that droops down low means your cat is not able to cope with something negative going on. Maybe the food you gave her is not quite right. A high tail, waving actively or just quivering, says she feels great, wants to let you know she is euphoric. A wildly-swinging tail suggests that you leave her to herself, that something is not just right in her world. Twitching? Your cat may feel you are saying something about her and is self-conscious. A cat is always aware of herself and her image and the Tail 'Attitude' demonstrates it. A bushy tail indicates a readiness to attack; combined with hisses and screeches, it adds up to a frightening look.

BODY 'ATTITUDE'

A high arched body means "stay away or be ready to fight". When her body is on an even keel, she holds up her head and approaches you; she is almost totally relaxed. It's a good time to talk to her. When feeling timid, she will approach in a partially sidewise stance. She needs reassurance and friendly talk. When a cat crouches down, she is either ready to admit defeat or submission, or is preparing to defend herself. When lying on her back, she is either inviting a person to scratch her stomach, indicating that she feels very secure, or that she defies the person to touch her, at which point, she may strike out with a protective paw, almost by instinct.

PAW 'ATTITUDE'

Cats have paws for protection and for use in handling prey. As kittens, paws are for playful moods, but care must be taken that they may not accidentally scratch a child or you. The paws are also used by the cat to embrace a person without the showing of claws. When used to 'bother' someone, i.e., tapping with her paws to get something faster, a cat usually succeeds. As a kitten, a cat's paws are used at the mother's breast, to 'knead' the mother's soft skin. It stimulates the flow of milk and makes both mother and baby feel more comfortable. (It's what a cat may do when sitting in your lap, recalling her nesting time, stroking the fabric of your clothing before settling down).

EYE 'ATTITUDE'

As poets say, eyes can express the soul of a human being. Eyes are the primary facial attributes of a cat's message to you. When they blink or wink, the eyes are signalling a special welcome greeting or saying that a lot has happened that day and, "I want to tell you all about it". When a cat's eyes are very large, something is frightening her or really upsetting her. When her eyes show narrow slits, a cat is in a business-like mode, analysing and reading your messages. Eyes half-closed indicate sleep-time or a cautious approach. Eyes that are wide open and looking right at you indicate that she is giving full attention to your conversation. She is waiting to hear your ideas or instructions. When her eyes appear to stare at you, your cat is in a confrontational mode. She is watching something or someone with readiness to defend herself. If a cat crouches down and her eyes do not stare, she is in a docile, receptive mode.

B. SOUND LANGUAGE

When nature created the cat, she forgot to include a set of instructions for every owner who would like to understand what his or her little companion wants, when she wants it. People speak one language, the cat another. But Nature did us a favour. She gave the cat the ability to communicate with people through a system of 'coded' messages, easy to translate if we will only stop to look.

There is one code to describe the way a cat uses her face (eyes, ears and head) to create the mood of the message, another code to explain the cat's body motions, a third to telegraph the message 'by tails'. Usually, these three codes work in perfect unison to tell a quick story. In addition, and at times equally important for interpreting a cat's message is the vocal or voice code.

Because the cat's vocal delivery can quickly identify the 'tone' or emotional impact of her communication, you will be able to determine the positive or negative tenor of her conversation simultaneously. Listen as she 'sings the blues' at one time, warns you of some impending danger with an 'alarm' in her voice, or asks for your attention and interest with a purring little 'love song' she writes and composes for you on the spot. These voice changes have a code of their own.

BACKGROUND TO A CAT'S VOCALISING

We must understand that cats do not

originate basic strategies as humans would. For example, in the architecting or engineering of a building, all work is done with cold logic and colder mathematics. Cats respond to their emotions and all their planning centres assist in finding emotional releases for their feelings. In mind and body, one can see how a cat, in all her watching and her cautious trial-and-error probing of people and things around her, is seeking some goal that is pleasing to her senses, complimentary to her ego, and satisfying to her physical and mental needs of the moment.

She is an all-out hedonist, living for the pleasures of today, for getting the absolute most for herself out of every human and non-human connection that each new day brings. If she awakens her human, it is with the thought that her breakfast will be ready sooner. If she experiences terror when it appears that her human, who is sleeping soundly, may be more than just sleeping, her panic involves having to find another human to take that one's place. Cats have an extraordinarily well-developed sense of what is best for them, at all times, and if it means being very nice to people and making them feel very comfortable to get what she wants, it is well worth the investment, by her way of thinking.

In this quid-pro-quo, feelings-on-the-surface world of cats, they go through their days revealing and staging their mental states, like itinerant bards, back in Shakespeare's time. Accordingly, these 'ham actors' and emoters love attention and live for the chance to show off talents to people who respond to them. They can get attention with their voices. They need to be loved by people. Again, their voices can help win that love.

A research project on cats in the mid-1940's revealed that a cat possesses a speaking vocabulary that includes five vowels, nine consonants and three diphthongs.

When this basic A-B-C structure is multiplied by the possible pitch and volume variations which the cat is capable of using, the total effective vocabulary of a cat becomes large enough to express several messages, addressed to other animals or to humans.

In a cat's vocal language, she uses six basic sound types. They include:

1. The 'hunting' call. A cat, looking out a window and seeing a bird on the lawn or in

a tree, will emit a staccato sound, unlike any other sound in the cat's repertoire. Every cat, street-bred or highly domesticated, uses it almost compulsively.

2. When a cat is in an angry and turbulent mood, the discordant cries are sometimes called 'caterwauling'. They occur most frequently at mating times, when two males will confront each other, or even when two spayed females argue over territories. These are the most irritating sounds to the human ear and are heard mostly in the early morning hours when most people want to sleep. These wild calls, stark reminders of every cat's jungle heritage, will increase in volume and ferocity as the cat's anger rises, and become lower on the sound scale as each episode in the fighting recedes. Some cat sound experts use terms like growling, wailing and howling in the same category with the sounds of timber wolves, howling at the moon, common to many different animal species.

3. At times when a cat is facing something quite frightening, her natural instinct is to

run away and get under cover. But if that is not possible, the next best defence is to utter a strange combination of 'yowls' that describes an animal with her back to the wall, willing to overcome her fear and to attack. Between the yowls, which can be heard at long distances, the cat will imitate the hissing of a trapped snake, ready to sink its fangs into an attacker. If it is a dog cornering the cat, this sound background and the cat's hunched and menacing body language are usually enough to send the attacker on his way.

4. When a cat is in pain, the response is a loud cry for help that is unmistakeable. It is more of a scream or shriek, which, once heard, cannot be compared to any other sound in a cat's repertoire. When a kitten experiences pain, it will squeal for help and is usually found and comforted by the mother cat. After leaving the nest, the same plaintive cry will signal for help to the cat's substitute mother, her owner.

5. Little kittens give out a meowing sound to get the attention of their mothers, and this basic sound becomes a variety of 'meows'

as the kitten grows into adulthood as a cat. The primary purpose of all these meows is to say, "Look at me . . . Look at me . . . Give me your attention!"

Cats can cry, plead, demand, complain and show affection with different tones and volumes of the same basic sounds. As they come to know the sounds of human language, they often alter their meowings as an arranger will adapt a musical piece to suit his or her own orchestration. Cats 'play it by ear' to get the results they want and never hesitate to try a new set of vocals that seems to work better.

If several phonetic specialists were given the same sound to interpret on a printed page, one might write a certain cat's sound like this: 'mmmhhhrrrnaaahooow . . .'

Another phoneticist may write: 'muurrraaahooommmrrraaa . . .' etc. What is important is that you train your ear to listen for the sounds that Your Talking Cat is using, realising that only by remembering *her* ways of talking, *her* ways of asking for what she wants will you achieve a realistic and practical mastery of vocal cat language.

Understand that all kittens raised in a

domestic setting are going to retain their kitten-like purr-sonalities and revert to their kitten ways more frequently than you may realise. Occasionally, in her role-playing, without your being aware of it, your kitten will become the 'mother' and you will become the kitten. Again, it makes for an interesting game, in which the 'rules' change constantly.

As you tune in to all these sounds, one will be saying, "Let me out!" (a soft "meeaahoo"); another, slightly higher when the cat is outside, will be "Let me in again!" ("meeeaaaoooh"). And still another accented "mmmmeeeowrrr" will demand attention. It will take you at least a few weeks to begin a working inventory of your cat's sounds and their meanings, but it is well worth the effort.

6.   The sound which most cat-owners like to hear is the PURR. Mostly, the sound of purring identifies a cat whose world is at peace and wants to show it. Purring is the most pleasing of cat sounds, although experts are not certain of exactly where in the cat's throat the sound originates. It is the cat's way, since her earliest days as a kitten, to 'let go' all of her instinctive

defences and to totally relax. It signifies a mood of accepting the world as a friend, of saying, "I have no hostility toward you."

Purring is first practised by a kitten at her mother's breast to confirm the fact that the kitten and mother are in perfect harmony with each other. It is the mother cat's way of letting the kittens know she is there and that everything is 'A-OK' . . . the cat's way of letting her master know that she accepts her position as a willing subordinate. It works for a male who wants to accept secondary social status to another male. It is a cat's 'white flag' of surrender to superior forces. It says, "I've put down all my weapons, let's be friends."

Purring appears to be the ultimate bonding device of a cat in her continuing efforts to accept the premise of civilisation. It has a salutary effect on cat and cat person to an equal degree.

YOUR TALKING KITTEN AND YOU

Every cat was once a kitten, the time of her life when she was almost totally cared for by her mother, when the hunt meant rolling a ball of yarn or nipping at a toy mouse, when the people she met would treat her like a little queen.

For some cats, that fun time may pass too quickly. Under the stress of urging by males to return to the action of the night world, or under the time stress of many neurotic mothers, kittens may be cast out of their habitats as early as two to three weeks. Some experts claim that this circumstance often develops some deep psychological problems in the young cat and reveals them later in various kinds of neuroses.

Normally, released cats may remain under their mother's care from 8 to 12 weeks, enough time to learn most of the things a kitten should know to face the complicated world of a full-grown cat.

During this period, the kittens and the mother have their own language by which the mother cat can call its offspring to "come for your dinner", "don't wander too far", "watch how I bathe you", etc. The mother cat reserves this 'first reader' language for kittens only, drops it when the litter is gone. In response, which almost everyone has heard, the kitten utters its tiny "meeeuuuus" that add to the appeal kitties have for humans of all ages.

C. TEST YOUR CAT LANGUAGE I.Q.

Can You Interpret What Each of These Talking Cats is Saying?

Now that you have a preliminary knowledge of the alphabet of cat language, the illustrations throughout this book will test your judgement in 'reading-a-cat' skills. The artist, who incidentally has a cat and loves it, was asked to visualise how a cat would appear when expressing certain moods or feelings.

You have seen similar 'situation photos' and captions in some of your favourite cat magazines. What this game does is to give you all the message clues and ask you to match them with the appropriate caption. In effect, it is what Your Talking Cat does, again and again, during its talks with you.

Your score of correctly-matched pictures and captions, as of today, will surely be improved a week later, after you've started to put your new powers of 'observation and interpretation' to work. Have fun!

The following captions express different moods and mental states which all cats experience. Each caption has a matching picture of a cat. No two pictures fit exactly any one caption. Correct answers appear on page 130.

1. "I ADORE YOU."
2. "YOU CALL THIS EDIBLE?"
3. "COME TO MUMMY, KITTENS!"
4. "TAKE OFF!"
5. "I'M STUDYING YOU."
6. "I'M CONTENT HERE."
7. "FORGET MY DINNER?"
8. "I KNOW THERE'S A MOUSE IN THIS HOUSE!"
9. "WHAT A WONDERFUL WORLD!"
10. "WHO IS THAT STRANGER?"
11. "PLAY BALL WITH ME?"
12. "LET ME OUT!"
13. "THIS IS MY PLACE."
14. "ANYBODY HOME?"
15. "I AM NOT AMUSED."
16. "LET ME MARK YOU."
17. "READY FOR A CHAT?"
18. "I'M STALKING MY PREY."
19. "YOU AGAIN?"
20. "ROMEO, OH ROMEO..."
21. "I'M SORRY."
22. "DON'T RUSH ME!"
23. "ARE YOU TALKING ABOUT ME?"
24. "WAKE ME FOR DINNER."
25. "I WANT MY MUMMY!"
26. "STATE YOUR BUSINESS!"

J

K

Chapter VII
This and That About Talking Cats

TALKING CAT STORY

There's the story of the frog and the scorpion who were trapped by a flood on a small island, cut off from the mainland. The scorpion convinced the frog that if the frog, which could swim, were to let him (the scorpion) on its back, both could be saved. The frog agreed, but halfway across the water, the scorpion stung the frog who cried: "Why did you do that, scorpion? Now we both die!" The scorpion replied: "But I'm a scorpion! What else could I do?"

Like the scorpion, Your Talking Cat was never intended by Nature to live in a warm house or to be fed nutritious food from tins opened by electric tin-openers. Your cat is designed to go out and kill a bird, a mouse or other small prey.

Your cat tries to tell you that, even demonstrates this urge to find its own live prey, even though the need is passed. For some people, this is a somewhat revolting feline habit, totally uncivilised.

MORAL OF THE STORY: Ask why of Mother Nature, not her cat.

LAP LANDERS

A cat really never grows up, even though it may be mature in years. One of a cat's most pleasant memories is the time it had with its mother, snug and safe under her protection. So, when a cat jumps up on her person's lap, it is a momentary return to being with her mother, ready to feed.

She will circle around, then settle down, pressing her paws down into the person's thighs, just as a kitten tamps down on the mother cat's belly to stimulate a greater flow of milk. But she is no longer a kitten and her claws may be sharp enough to disturb the person, who may respond by pushing her back to the floor. This can be very confusing to the cat who cannot comprehend why this surrogate mother would ever do something like that to her infant!

A knowledgeable person will understand the cat's seemingly odd behaviour in this lap ritual and let the cat complete its lap-circling and tamping ritual. She finally will stop and curl up contentedly, with a soothing purr to match. To communicate successfully with a cat, one must remember the completely different species of creature she represents and tolerate behaviour that appears totally non-human at times, which it is.

Your Talking Cat has a good reason for the things she does, based on her origins and her natural linkage to another and uncivilised world. The transition is never easy.

Y

THE GIVER

A cat has ways of showing its appreciation for the loving care and kindness which a family will heap upon it. Occasionally, a cat will bring home something which it considers of value and drop it at the feet of her owner. She says wordlessly: "This gift shows how much I think of you. Thank you for all you do for me!"

The gift could even be a fresh-killed bird or mouse – the ultimate gift gesture of a proud cat. Some bright cats will bring the gift over to your freezer to be stored as a future meal!

COMMUNICATING FEAR

Before your cat fights, she first tries to avoid fighting by intimidating her opponent, animal or human. First, her brain signals her body to look bigger by puffing up her tail and furry coat. At the same time, the cat arches her back to appear larger. Her ears are in battle formation, close to the head. Her eyes are wide open and large, fixed hypnotically on the enemy. Then, with her long, sharp teeth showing ominously, ready to lock into a vulnerable neck, she emits frightening hisses, almost like the sounds of a rattler about to strike. The scenario is often enough to get any attacker to back away – fast!

CATS AND COMMUNICATIONS

Jealousy, anger, hurt feelings, jubilation and depression are a cat's heritage as much as a human's. For example, a cat that has been the star pet in its environment may feel very jealous of a new pet or a new baby in the house. She may decide to leave for days at a time to show her displeasure. Soon, missed meal-times, frightening situations and general home-sickness send her back into the family circle and she accepts her new place in a changed environment. Most cats can rationalise a changed image, extracting the best out of a momentarily negative situation.

MADE FOR EACH OTHER

Probably the best thing that could ever happen to a person who wants a very bright and interesting companion would be the adoption of a pet cat. At the same time, the best thing ever for a people-liking cat would be to meet that cat-seeking person. This mutual fulfilment of deep needs for friendship is something magical, something money cannot buy.

Obviously, for millions of cats' families throughout Great Britain, the United States, France, Germany, Italy, Switzerland, Belgium and other countries, the arrangement is working out almost flawlessly. Long live this cat-human friendship!

THAT'S THE RUB

Cats have special kinds of greetings for people they like, especially for their owners. For example, a cat may come over to you and rub her head and body against your legs and wrap her tail around your ankle in a friendly gesture. This is one of the most personal of all cat rituals, involving the three primary scent glands – on her forehead, on the side of her mouth and at the base of her tail. She will go through this routine many times, satisfied that she has left her scent on you and in the process has picked up your scent on her fur.

Of course, the scents she leaves are too delicate for us to detect, but they are there, none-the-less. After leaving, she will sit down and start 'tasting' the scents you left on her body, licking them off her fur meticulously. It adds to the intimacy of her relations with you and strengthens the bonds of companionship between you. On your part, by stroking her softly, while holding up your other hand for her to rub against and lick, you will have shown the fondness you have for her in return. It motivates her to continue the rubbing and nuzzling.

When your cat does this to a stranger in your house, it is for the purpose of identifying the person on the next visit, and to use another 'living messenger' to deliver her special scents to the next cat that person may encounter. What better communications system than that?

WHY CATS RESENT BEING STARED AT

A cat does not think with logic as people are presumed to think. She thinks with her emotions and responds to situations involving animals or people in a defensive, emotional manner. When a person stares at her, her radar immediately puts her on alert, identifying the person with possible threat to her well-being.

It reflects the instinctive animal reaction of a jungle animal who feels that an enemy is doing surveillance on her, in exactly the same way that she watches and stares at her prey, an unfortunate bird or rodent.

In associating stares with danger, you may find her reaction the same as when meeting any other possible aggressor: she may walk away or display her own most intimidating body language, including a snake-like hissing sound.

OVER-COMMUNICATION

In some sections of the cat world, as many as 2,000 cats live within a square-mile radius. In the United States alone, an estimated 50 million-plus cats eat, drink, mate and sleep in homes or on the streets. That's 200 million padded paws, ready and able to pounce on a rodent population many times that number. Without the excellent work of animal shelters, vets and other animal-care organisations, the Talking Cat population could multiply in geometric progression, with more zeroes than most national debts.

Unless you pay undivided attention to her when she comes over to talk with you, there is an eventual breakdown of communications which may become difficult to renew.

Under the pressures of time we all face today, it may be a higher priority to complete your newspaper, make some social telephone calls, sit down at the piano or do any of a number of things, all meaningless to your cat.

But when she begins to sense that your 'private and personal' time with her is getting briefer and briefer, that you are permitting more and more distractions to break into *her* time, she may begin to withdraw and sulk. It happens between people. It happens between Your Talking Cat and you.

As an analogy, think of a woman who spends all her waking hours taking care of her little children, waiting for her husband to return from work to discuss the day's events. If he chooses, night after night, to avoid conversation with her, focussed on a television screen or doing his office homework, something starts happening to the relationship.

Understandably, a sensitive, comfort-and-affection seeking cat feels the same way, locked in a room all day, waiting for your return.

You can correct that problem easily with a sincere show of interest, real concentration on the 'Primer of Cat Language' and a little

I

C

genuine companionship. Do that consistently for 15 minutes a day and Tabby will release you to the telephone, the piano, newspaper or bridge game, with no problem. Correction: *Maybe* she'll release you!

SILENT BALLOT COMMUNICATION

It may be difficult for someone with two kittens to understand why one kitten will try to dominate the other, even pummelling her brother or sister with paw blows and acting the bully, generally, while the other kitten remains passive and accepts humiliation. The fact is *that's the way cats are.*

In the very competitive world of cats (and people), there will be personalities born more aggressive and assertive than others. In an unstated army system of rank, the mother cat is the total and final court of appeal; the most aggressive cat is in the next position of authority; the 'assistant' to him or her is next; down to the 'privates' at the bottom of the totem pole.

In selecting a leader, a group of cats will choose by silent ballot, not necessarily the largest among them, but the cat with *the most charisma.* He, or she, does not have to bully anyone, to prove his, or her, leadership; he, or she, *is just accepted as a matter of natural selection.* It is almost the way people accept their political leaders, sometimes wisely, sometimes not so wisely.

MOUSERS

It's the name used even in our times for cats, particularly in rural areas where grain storage bins and barns need protection from rodents. These are some of the hardest-working cats in the world, and the happiest. They communicate mostly with a pounce and a quick bite.

ESP? TELEPATHY? VERY POSSIBLY

The cat's super-sensitive nervous system, joined functionally with a large brain in proportion to her size, has convinced many people that she possesses extra-sensory perception (ESP). Actually, a cat's five senses – sight, hearing, touch, taste and smell – are so highly-developed by evolution that human beings will probably never catch up to them in these attributes. In only one instance, eyesight in daytime, can a person's eyes out-perform those of a cat.

It is through these senses that a cat is able to detect earthquake tremors long before the catastrophe happens, is able to smell smoke before a fire-detector, and can hear the approach of possible intruders before an electronic alarm can give a warning.

All these hyper-sensitive, lightning-fast response mechanisms that make up the highly-efficient anatomy of a cat serve her at the same time as a first-rate communications centre.

THE 'CAT'S WHISKERS' AS COMMUNICATORS

These delicately-designed 'sensors' are essential to the cat's system of communications. Each whisker, located on the face, above the eyes and behind the front leg, has a microscopic nerve-ending that helps guide the cat through poorly visible underbrush, around rocks and other obstructions, and more important, adds to the cat's night vision on hunting expeditions.

CAT 'COMMUNICATION' WITH A MOUSE

The instinctive talent passed along by mother cats over thousands of generations of cats, the talent for being the four-legged nemesis of disease-bearing rodents, is a study in natural efficiency.

When Mother Nature designed one of Darwin's most apt and versatile 'survivors', she created a marvellous hunter, combined with an equally marvellous species of household pet.

If you were to make a film of a cat, from the start of her mouse-entrapment to the final scene, your production would embrace six episodes: 1) Stalking Time; 2) Slinking Time; 3) Crouching Time (Ambush); 4) Leaping Time; 5) Trapping Time and, finally, 6) Goodbye Mouse Time.

These successive actions, which appear so simple to the eye, so obvious from an analytical standpoint, have been formulated and synchronised over a million or more years to become one of the great animal wonders of the world.

It is with great innate pride that a healthy and natural cat carries this little time-piece of destruction within her mind and body. She is subliminally aware of these skills at all times, and one of her proudest gifts of action to her human companion is to demonstrate for her person this unique, and to her, exciting performance.

Again, anyone who would care to alter nature's way, i.e., to chastise a cat for 'doing it naturally', would be like trying to tamper with the laws of our Universe. It's far better to accept a love-giving cat for what she is, rather than ask her to be something you wish she were.

HOW A CAT SAYS "LOOK AT ME"

Cats are the *ultimate watchers*. They learn about the tangible world of their people and their cars, refrigerators, vacuum-cleaners, toasters and microwave ovens that civilisation has created for the creature comforts and conveniences of their households. They watch, learn and decide what parts of this environment are important and which are not.

Tangibles are easier to understand, especially for a cat, whose entire life revolves around the visible and touchable things to which she responds negatively and positively.

Now comes the time when your cat watches you at work on mysterious *intangibles*, such as sheets of paper that rustle and books that scarcely make a sound as you turn the pages.

Your cat, one of the world's most curious of animals, cannot quite fathom why these objects can keep you so entertained that you may not even notice her. In fact, anything you do that appears to focus all your attention becomes immediately interesting to her, too.

Invariably, Your Talking Cat, hungry to learn, will come over to compete for attention, or at least try to understand what is keeping you so silently intent.

If the day should arrive when a cat can be taught to read a newspaper or magazine, to understand what is going on in a television situation comedy, it will be because, by Darwin's theory, *the cat wants to know*, and Mother Nature may eventually give her the means to know.

MASTER OR PET . . . WHICH AM I?

Cats are generally known for their aloofness and complete unawareness of the instructions or commands of those around them.

An extreme example of this almost total feeling of self esteem can, in many instances, leave a cat confused as to which one, the human being or herself, is in charge. In other words, she may feel, at times, like the one responsible for the care of the person charged to her. It then becomes her (the cat's) job to remind the person when to serve breakfast or dinner, when to awaken, when to be let outside, etc. It's one of the most amusing cases of megalomania on record. When it occurs, a cat may suddenly swing its tail back and forth, in time with its disconnecting thoughts.

PERSON-TO-PERSON

A cat likes to do her communicating on a one-to-one, private basis. When your home begins to be shared by other pets, Your Talking Cat may retreat for awhile, waiting for the opportunity to talk with you alone. By rule of thumb, cats in multi-pet homes will not communicate as frequently as before the new troops arrived. It's logical that they begin to converse more among themselves, with a slightly different and faster rate of delivery.

COMMUNICATING BY BIRTHDAYS

Can a cat communicate with your birthdays? In their limited number of years, compared to the life-span average of humans, the numbers

S

N

relate on the following scale:
- year one for a cat equals year 15 for a human;
- year two for a cat equals year 25 for a human;
- year four for a cat equals year 40 for a human;
- year 10 for a cat equals year 60 for a human;
- year 15 for a cat equals year 75 for a human;
- year 20 for a cat equals year 105 for a human.

CAT-TO-CAMERA COMMUNICATIONS

No breed of pet is more natural in front of a camera lens than a cat. A cat is a born model, with her great, expressive face, her big, hungry eyes, her ability to 'ham it up' as a performer, her wide range of emotional responses – all perfect to photograph. A cat-owner without a camera always handy is like a cinema without popcorn.

'TUNNELS OF FUN' GAMES

Since they first roamed the earth, cats have been stalkers of field mice and other small rodents, frequently holed up in deep, underground tunnels. Sometimes a cat will try to enter one of these underground nests and finds itself caught in the tunnel.

But the fascination of tunnels haunts a cat, as

if in a dream, all through its life. It's one reason why some people have constructed little tunnel parks for their cats made from safe, terracotta drain-pipes you can buy in most building supply centres. Be sure that the pipes are large enough for your cat to crawl through without being trapped. Don't make any section more than four or five feet long to be sure that you can reach your cat at either end. If outdoors, add scenery with a growth of plants and rocks to provide realistic mini-jungle atmosphere. It's a great place for Your Talking Cat to play 'hide-and-seek' with you because she loves to be a little pixie at times, as most kids (and grown-up kids) enjoy being occasionally.

NO HIGH ANXIETY

Watch the way Your Talking Cat goes about estimating her moves, when on some high ledge or counter, planning to descend to floor-level safety. She thinks like an athlete, preparing to scale a bar in the pole vault event, or like a professional baseball player estimating the speed and distance of a baseball coming in her direction.

Her reflexes and judgement of height and

distance are nothing short of miraculous. Within a micro-second, she may release her claws to slow down the fall along the edge of a cabinet and then rebound to the floor softly, every muscle and ligament of every leg joint helping to reduce the impact. Remember that a five-foot drop for a cat would be the equivalent of a 25-foot drop (or more) for a man!

INSTANT NEUTRALISER

When a mother cat is carrying one of her kittens, she gently takes it in her mouth by the thick and loose fur behind its neck. Not only does it not hurt the kitten at all, it also tends to act as a sedative, since it cuts off part of the sensory action along the kitten's spine. A vet sometimes grasps the same portion of an adult cat's neck and shoulder, and instantly reduces the cat's nervousness on the examination table.

HAVE TIME, WILL TRAVEL

Talking cats like to travel with their families once all the fear of travel is removed. That means getting your cat accustomed to the idea of going from place to place in her carrier.

A cat likes to be sure of where she is at all

times, needs calm, 'motherly' talk to soothe her nerves, and mild stroking to reduce her fears.

Important pre-trip considerations include vaccinations; I.D. tags; advance reservations at places that accept cats; bringing along a supply of home water to avoid stomach problems; and not feeding your cat for at least six hours before the trip begins.

Make sure you bring along her favourite bed and litter box. Keep car windows slightly open. Be aware that sometimes a cat will jump into the road on seeing another cat, dog or bird. With one trip under her belt, however, Tabby may become a seasoned traveller.

If you're travelling by air, be sure to get all the advance details from your airline agent.

CATS AND DOGS AS PETS

Dogs have been trained for domestic companionship longer than cats. They have been bred for centuries to obey their masters and often to perform specific, productive duties, e.g., the English Sheep Dog, the German Police Dog, the Golden Retriever Hunting Dog.

Over the centuries, the dog has learned to live in a civilised environment, motivated by being willing and able to serve a master, almost unqualifiedly.

A dog usually submits to his master's requests without questioning motives or reasons. Most of its wild-dog heritage has been 'cooled down' by people.

Cats, on the other hand, retain more of their wild instincts and ways. They have accepted human conveniences when it has suited their temporary needs. But most cats want the right to walk away from people and situations which displease them. They maintain open minds on deciding whom they like, whom they disdain. They insist on 'splitting their loyalties' between the comforts of a home and the excitement of the hunt.

You can always read a friendly dog. You can't always read a momentarily friendly cat. It makes life interesting.

A NAME IS A NAME

You'll find that cat names can be among the most creative subjects in our times. Dreaming up the exactly right name for a family cat may take days, even weeks, before every member of the family has a chance to put his or her special name up for a vote. Even the youngest member of a family, a three-year-old or a four-year-old, will fight to get a name chosen and, no matter what the family decision, may stubbornly call the cat by his or her choice. It is one of the most democratic processes remaining in our culture. Its preservation is critical.

MECHANICALLY INCLINED

Did you know that a cat can learn to lift a latch, tinkle a mailbox flap, push open a door, or climb a window to communicate its need to its owner? It learns these ingenious tricks by repeated observation and trial-and-error persistence.

BELL-RINGER

A bell attached to a cat's collar means that the owner would like to know where the cat is, as often as possible, and that he (or she) would like to help prevent the untimely demise of some unlucky bird, for example. After all, a cat is a natural predator and will kill for food or sport. The bell warns off a cat's prey.

HIGH PLACES

Why do some cats find some of the highest places in the home to curl up and sleep? Beside an instinct to sleep out of the reach of danger, they prefer places that provide maximum privacy and minimum disturbance by family members.

HIDE-AND-SEEK

A cat prefers to stay out of sight as much as possible. It finds dark corners and hidden places around the home to which it can retreat when an active family becomes too noisy or annoying. It may find a snug and virtually unseen spot under a sink, behind a couch, or in an open storage cupboard. Because of this habit, thousands of cats are injured or die each year because they chose the wrong places to rest, like under a car, on machinery, etc. Be alert and watch out for them.

THE HUNTER

The most domesticated cat is still basically a wild creature, bound by natural instincts to the jungles and forests which its breed once inhabited. When a household cat spots a bird in a tree or on the lawn, no matter what the cat may be doing, you will see it crouch down, low to the ground, become totally alert, ears erect, eyes fully open, and ready for the day's catch. At these moments, its human companions in conversation realise that Mother Nature is a cat's first mistress, the one who can whisper cat language instructions into her brain at almost any time. We are merely her assigned caretakers.

FAMILIAR SOUNDS

Cats are smart enough to know the different motor sounds of cars driven by two members of the family. They know the purr-son who is arriving the moment the car enters the driveway.

Once a cat has fixed a sound in its mind, it knows the meaning of the sound. For example, the dropping of a shoe, the clink of a spoon against a porcelain cup or a metal pot, a purr-son humming in the shower, the drip of a tap, or the whirr of a tin-opener. In each instance, it relates the sound to something purr-sonal for her – her food being dished out, her greeting to someone she loves, or her signal to join a favourite kid going to bed.

SWEET LESSON

Other domestic animals will gratefully accept bits of chocolate or other sweets. A cat will not, if it is consistent with its breed. Protein tid-bits are always to its liking, especially if they feature one or more of the same trio – fish, meat or fowl.

PRESIDENTS ARE CAT PEOPLE, TOO

Not many people know that several of the most famous US Presidents had cat companions in the White House.

While no record of a pet cat is in any of the first President's personal papers, George Washington had a tiny trapdoor set into the wall of the third floor of his mansion in Mount Vernon, suggesting that he may have had a cat there.

Abraham Lincoln loved cats and would play with them for hours in his home in Illinois. When Lincoln's sons, Tad, who had a dog, and Willie, who had a cat, announced that puppies and kittens had been born on the same day,

Lincoln was overjoyed and proceeded to give names to all the newcomers.

President Theodore Roosevelt had two cats – 'Slippers' and 'Tom Quartz'.

Calvin Coolidge had two cats in the White House, called 'Tiger' and 'Blacky'.

John F. Kennedy's daughter, Carolyn, had a cat which she called 'Tom Kitten'.

Both President Gerald Ford and President Jimmy Carter were cat lovers.

(From *Cat Fancy Magazine*, July 1991).

SOME BORN MORE EQUAL THAN OTHERS

No two humans are exactly alike, genetically or personality-wise. Neither are cats.

That is why some cats make better 'talkers' than others, are more willing to communicate with people, and more willing to accommodate themselves to domestic life and its daily routines.

Some cats are considerably more intelligent than others and find the challenge of dialogue with people irresistible.

Some cats are very neurotic and will go through minor emotional breakdowns, on occasion, to get what they want. Other cats rarely kick up a fuss, are 'street smart' and cool, even in the face of danger.

Some cats need human response and friendship most of the time. Other cats love their freedom so much that coming back home for a 'people break' is only a nice change of pace.

So don't make the mistake of expecting Your Talking Cat to follow any pattern suggested in books. A smart cat may sense that you're trying to 'type it' and perversely rewrite all the expert's rules of thumb.

A CAT AND A 2-YEAR-OLD

Books on child-care remind mothers and other members of the family that during the second year after birth, a child becomes self-assertive, stubborn, and rebellious about almost any request from his elders.

A cat is like that most of the time, especially during her early years. When you want a "Yes" answer, it's "No!" and reflects the cat's instinct for independence at all costs.

NO YESTERDAY, NO TOMORROW

All of a cat's involvements happen in an

T

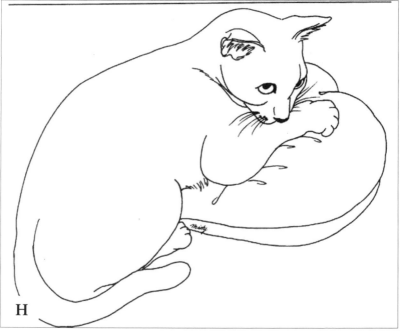

H

immediate time-frame. Only what she can touch, smell, see or experience right now has any meaning to her. She eats now, plays now, relieves herself now, goes out to find a mate now and comes back home now.

When she wants to talk to you, it's now, not later. No calendars or diaries concern a cat. On that basis, it's relaxing for humans to stop once in a while and think as a cat thinks – Now!

BALANCING ACT

Ever think of the wonderfully-balanced look of a cat as she walks along the narrow edge of a fence? Watch the way her legs are exactly lined up, the way her tail swings left and right. While a squirrel, with its shorter front legs, has the advantage in some outdoor stunts, cats are more beautiful to watch.

FAMOUS SAYINGS AND CATS

Cats have inspired many novelists and poets over the years but, mostly, cats are the centre of attention in sayings the world over.

Following are explanations for lines known to every school child:

'When the cat's away, the mice will play.'

Meaning: When an authority is gone, people take advantage of the fact.

'Curiosity once killed a cat.'

Meaning: Since cats are always poking around new places, danger could be lurking.

'Cats like fish but never get wet feet.'

Meaning: One must take some chances if success is to be won.

'A cat has nine lives.'

Meaning: Cats take very good care of themselves, land on their feet in a big fall; they must lead charmed lives.

FREE PUBLICITY

World-wide promotion of the hit musical show *Cats*, with a box-office record on Broadway, has done great things for the cat populations of several countries. It humanised the lives of cats at various age levels and helped popularise the joys of cat ownership to the point where there are now more 'cat families' than 'dog families', according to a recent survey. One practical reason may be that in urban communities, a cat is more capable than a dog of taking care of itself in the absence of its owner, who may be at work all day.

OTHER CAT MATTERS

From their earliest moments of play, kittens enjoy the fun of 'play-fighting'. They tumble, roll over, jump on or over their opponents, and do everything active but hurt each other. As they grow, with the possibility of serious accidents, they restrain their actions.

As they begin to practise for their natural roles as rodent-killers, dozens of different toys enter the picture, most inspired by the 'cat-and-mouse' theme. Whether it's a ping-pong ball, a rubber ball or a cloth catnip-filled mouse, the toy takes on a training function, helping prepare the cat for the job of rodent-stalking and bird-chasing. It is probably the most blood-thirsty kind of play ever invented, because the cat's favourite trick is to toy with her plaything mouse until she finally grasps it firmly between her paws and administers the cat's famous coup de gras.

Lightweight, home-made 'toys', including aluminium foil balls, tissue paper balls, empty cotton reels, or champagne bottle corks, all obviously delight a young cat 'mouse warrior'.

Because by nature the cat is able to reach into a stream and, with one paw, flip a fish onto the land and eat it, little cloth fish make her as happy as does a little cloth mouse.

Imaginative cat-owners have succeeded in playing games with their pets that demonstrate an amazing ability of cats to learn games of a higher mental order. For example, one man taught his cat to imitate the trained circus tigers and jump from chair to chair on command with a tiny three-inch 'circus whip' and a 'trainer's T-shirt' for showmanship.

One musician trained his cat to pick out favourite notes on an electric organ and actually write 'cat music'!

Your Talking Cat is a treasure trove of great entertainment. Both you and your cat will enjoy the challenge of inventing new 'communicating' games.

A kitten, as well as an older cat in her 'second childhood', can find as much or more pleasure in chasing a ping-pong ball, rolling an empty spool across the kitchen floor, chasing down a fast-moving sun-spot on the wall, flipping around and biting a rubber mouse or fish, slapping and chasing a tennis ball hung from a chair, than she might find in the most ingeniously-designed and costly toy. It's your personal involvement in your cat's play that she really wants most. You are her 'mother purr-son' in all she does and at play, too. She wants to show off for *you*!

To get you involved in a challenging game is one of a cat's favourite pastimes. Simple 'fetching' is a favourite, especially if a little ball rolls under the bed or sofa and requires ingenuity to find.

Another game involves placing a small handkerchief or piece of coloured cloth on the floor or on an end-table and challenging your cat to grab it with her paw before you do with your fingers. You study her eyes and she studies yours to see who will be quickest on the draw.

Another version is to hold out your palm and see if your cat can tap it with her paw before you pull it away. Then, she must hold out her paw and you must tap it before she can pull it back. Remarkably, an intelligent cat can learn this game within one or two sessions of teaching.

OPEN LETTER FROM A TALKING CAT

Dear Reader,

We live in a very fast-paced world, as you know. Sometimes, because of time pressures, we may overlook all 'the little things' that make and keep a friendship with your cat.

Maybe your cat is talking to you, trying to tell you how she feels today, and you are much too absorbed with other things to stop for a while and really pay attention with some of your 'best' time.

A

This book was written in the hope that your life may be enriched by a little closer friendship with your favourite cat, who may have been patiently storing up a lot of interesting things to tell you.

To do that, of course, you may need a little more tutoring in the fine points of Cat Language. In primer form, this book first asks you to STOP, LOOK and LISTEN. It may surprise you to learn that your intelligent little companion has some things of great value to tell you, *maybe even about yourself.*

So the next time Your Talking Cat ambles over to you, looks up and says: "Do you have a moment to sit and talk with me?", why not click off the VCR or TV, or put down that great mystery novel, or wind up the telephone conversation and look down pleasantly at her and say: "*Why sure, Kitty! Tell me what's on your mind.*" Then we'll *know* that you've enjoyed her company.

Your Talking Cat

W

L

Chapter VIII
The Fun Side
of Talking Cats

TALKING CAT MIND-READING GAME

Consider what a cat would be telling you if she could speak English and think in English with the same mastery of words and sentences that you have!

The statements on the following pages were written after looking into the faces of different cats of different ages at different times. They will release your own powers of observation and interpretation, as well as those of your friends, who may well compete in a parlour game to invent the most appropriate cat soliloquies.

Even the most expert of experts will admit that reading the mind of a cat is virtually impossible with our present scientific devices.

But suppose there were such equipment, and we could attach harmless electronics to a cat and watch the screen report what a typical, silent cat really thinks about.

It sure is fun chewing on this slipper of yours. Yes, it will probably get me into plenty of hot water, but if you were a kitten, wouldn't you get attention like this? Is there a better way?

You look so contented there on the couch with that thing you call a book in your hand. You know I can't read and the least you could do is to let me hear what's got you so interested. I think I'll jump on you and the book to let you know how I feel.

I heard a mouse in that wall last night and I think this is where it comes out. Nothing is as much fun as scaring the daylights out of one. And then, the coup de gras!

Why am I curled up in this corner where the kids can't find me? Didn't you ever have a hangover? I had a very active night, you know, out there in the backyard. Give me a break, won't you all?

That's my sleeping basket, old buddy! I'm a territorial cat, you know. And what's mine is mine!

Can't a gal wash up without you kids always staring at me? Didn't you ever see anybody licking away dirt before?

When that dumb dog gets off that nice warm chair, I'm gonna go for it! Maybe the doorbell will ring.

I don't like these jungle pictures. Can't you watch a ball game or something? Big cats like that scare the daylights out of me!

Of course, I like to watch a bowl of goldfish! You would, too, if you were a cat. I'm a natural sushi lover, you know.

Watch my eyes. I can hardly keep them open. That's how boring it is for me to watch you shuffle all those pieces of paper.

What's an income tax, anyway?

I don't like you to watch me out of that kitchen window. Sure, I'm stalking a nice, plump sparrow up in that tree. I'm only a cat, you know. And this is something cats do.

I'm sitting here and I'm not moving off this sofa for any of your guests coming in here! That's my final answer and don't be looking at me like that ... Hey ... don't you dare pick me up, master or no master.

You had me put up with a smelly, stupid dog in the house for two years now and you want me to welcome a baby, too? Don't you have any consideration for me at all? By the way, what's a baby?

What kind of nasty trick can I play on her tonight to show how much I miss her all day in that office place. Maybe I'll get up on top of the bookcase and when she opens the door ... Surprise!

If that kid insists on calling me all kinds of cute names and making like I'm a ball of fuzzy yarn, he's going to get a nice surprise! Maybe a cute little nip!

Wow, what a beautiful girl! Your taste is sure improving, my friend. Think I'll just go over there and put my scent on her stockings! I'll wait till you're out in the kitchen mixing drinks because you sure can be a poor sport.

I have to share a single human in this place with all these other cats. Doesn't she know I get very jealous? Doesn't she know that a cat can get very depressed with a gang of cats around all the time looking for attention, too?

TALKING CAT INTERVIEWS

At the present rate of scientific advances, it may be conceivable for cats and people to converse on a much higher plane. At that point, one might conjecture that some rather remarkable interviews could be recorded. Herewith, we venture a few typical examples:

X

E

CAT INTERVIEWS

Saki, a Japanese Cat, Visiting America

Q. How do you compare Far Eastern cats and their nine lives with the way cats live here?

A. "Not much different from the life-style in any Japanese city. Same bad air, same go, go, go, same human rat race. But I think we prepare fish more deliciously, if my nose doesn't fool me. And you know what you can do with all your fast-food..."

At An International Cat Show

Q. I understand that you are one of the two per cent of cats with cat-show breeding. Do you ever wish you were just another ordinary cat?

A. "My dear, it's noblesse oblige, you know. I'm so standoffish. Sometimes I decide not to answer my dinner-bell. A matter of family pride, you see. Keeps my weight down, too."

Ephram On A Farm

Q. Do you see a real difference between country cats and city cats?

A. "You bet your cornstalks! We work here, you know. Caught me twelve little fellows already this morning. Some of those city cats never even saw a decent-size mouse. We live longer, too."

Sammie, Urban Dweller

Q. How would you compare your life with the life of a country cat?

A. "Just no comparison, huh! Those hayseed mousers can't match anything we have here! It's the night-life for me, in a city like this. Maybe those mousers live longer, but maybe it only seems longer."

Frenchie, Paris

Q. Would you ever consider living somewhere less glamorous and exciting? Perhaps retiring to a horse stable?

A. "Monsieur, you must be joking! To be a cat, and in the shadow of the Eiffel Tower, who could ever want more, especially zee nightclubs in Gay Paree?"

Egbert, London

Q. How goes it with you, old chap?

A. "Just fine, thank you. And I'd say things are good down at the Exchange, too. Much better scraps lately. Even had a little filet mignon last night."

Chapter IX
Talking Cat Purr-sonals

How a cat can communicate geographically with her established home is a subject that has confounded many scholars.

'Smokey'

A friend tells of a special cat that lived happily in the entrance of an apartment complex in the middle of a very exclusive village. Everyone knew the cat and loved him. They called him 'Smokey' because of the grey-black colour of his fur. Tenants would feed him and he would talk to them, sharing all the news of each day's happenings.

Even though 'Smokey' knew that a lot of what he told them was going in one ear and out the other, both the talker and his audience enjoyed the conversations. 'Smokey', added my friend, was so outgoing, you'd think you were talking with a dog. Then came a day when the apartment building owner decided to evict 'Smokey', who was a nonpaid doorman, 'for aesthetic reasons'. He arranged to have 'Smokey' put in a box and transported somewhere two towns away.

"We really missed `Smokey's' greeting to us every morning and night when we returned from work", said my friend. "For three days, it was as if we had just said goodbye to a wonderful old friend. Then, on the fourth morning, there was `Smokey', back in the entrance, sleeping off his long trip back home! How did he manage it? No one knows, but we always said `Smokey' was a special kind of cat."

Again, the owner of the building made plans to eliminate 'Smokey'. This time, my friend, with the help of his wife, both of whom love animals, arranged to have 'Smokey' spayed and adopted by a lady who loves cats and had one who needed a companion. It has proven to be one of the happiest cat stories ever.

'Inky'

Cats often communicate with amazing ingenuity. This true story is about a cat called 'Inky', who was named for her jet-black colour.

'Inky' devised her own method of asking to

be let into the house. When a meow would fail to rouse the family, she would lift the brass letter slot flap at the base of the front door with her paw, letting it 'clink' gently against the matching brass frame. It always worked, and 'Inky' trained the family to listen for that 'clink' from then on.

'Inky' also was a thoughtful cat who would walk her little girl mistress to her school bus every morning, then return home. To watch little Nancy bathe, 'Inky' would perch atop a radiator in the bathroom. Sometimes it was uncomfortable and a little too hot, so 'Inky' devised signals and sounds that meowed her discomfort to the girl's mother, even hinting that a small towel, placed between her and the radiator top, would work fine. She made her point successfully. 'Inky' was a real communicator.

Rosalie, a young writer who has five cats, offered to contribute a few of her personal experiences, and they are included here. She writes:

"Don't Forget to Wash Behind the Ears, Dear!"

Perhaps because she was denied her own

shot at motherhood, 'Puma' is the self-appointed nurturer of her fellow-feline housemates (and, on many occasions, her non-feline owner, as well).

As the quasi-official matriarchal figure, she unselfishly devotes herself to the arduous tasks of ear-grooming and face-washing of the other cats. She gives them no choice but to sit patiently as she gently, but firmly, holds them down with her forearm for this ritual.

When 'Chessie' joined us as a tiny, abandoned street urchin, it was 'Puma' who instinctively offered her comfort. A year and a half later, the bonding between the two is apparent, as they are often seen cuddled together on, appropriately enough, the love-seat.

Perched above me on the back of the couch, 'Puma' takes it upon herself to oversee my 'grooming' as well, making sure she has tended to my eyelids, eyebrows, forehead and hair. Maybe she feels the need to return the care I provide for her. Nonetheless, I am touched by her giving gesture of love.

Catty Behaviour

Kitty wouldn't, couldn't tolerate me; she

didn't even attempt to hide her resentment of me intruding on HER territory. Any attempts at forming an alliance with her were met with haughty indifference.

When I sat next to Jon on the couch, there she was, ready to promptly wedge herself between us in order to gaze lovingly and adoringly at him. Apparently, she was trying to wedge herself between us in more ways than one.

Gradually, she realised that I was going to be around for awhile and, whether she liked it or not, she was going to have to share Jon. But I'm sure that in her own proud feline fashion, Kitty rationalised that by granting me official approval, she was automatically doubling the share of love and affection she received.

In His Own Way

Secret Cat Bye-Law: At any given time, the role of a cat-owner can, and will, be questioned, revoked or annulled by official whim of the cat itself.

When I was four, I was friends with my neighbour, Suzy, who lived, in my opinion, in Utopia. Besides having every toy advertised on 'The Flintstones', she had not one, but SIX cats. Since I was not permitted to have anything more than a goldfish, this boggled my pre-school mind.

Perhaps in need of a break from such a large cat establishment, 'Jerry', an orange-and-white tomcat, often would walk me home across the street. He never seemed to be in much of a hurry to return to his own domicile, however. In fact, he seemed to thrive on being something of a novelty to my brother and me, as we doted upon him and otherwise 'oohed' and 'aahed'.

The increasing amount of time 'Jerry' spent with us was so obvious that my friend and her family became somewhat miffed. Suzy's mother often marched her over to retrieve him, as if it would do any good.

Gradually, 'Jerry' became more and more comfortable with the idea of our home as his home. Brazenly, he would try to enter through any open door, or stare us down through the living-room window from the flower box. My parents knew they were beaten. They were about to become pet-owners by choice: not their choice, mind you, but that of a cat; one who was owned by someone else, no less.

I'm not sure at what point we truly became his, as it were. Perhaps when I began calling him 'Bootsie' because of his white paws, or when we bought him his first box of Friskies, the one with the orange cat on the front. Or maybe it was when my parents relented and let him in our house, something they vowed never to do. I think I know when. During a heated argument with Suzy, she picked up 'Bootsie' and walked out with him, proclaiming, "'Jerry' is really OUR cat and you just stole him." As soon as they crossed the street, he struggled from Suzy's arms, clawing her in the process, and ran back to this sobbing little girl who loved him.

Did we really 'steal' him? He was free to go back at any time, but he chose to be with us, where he could sleep on my bed day and night. He was pushed around in a doll carriage and covered with a blanket in a little doll crib.

It had started with a visit, but it lasted nine years. And only his final passing would ever let him leave us for good. 'Bootsie' enriched my childhood with his whimsical, endearing and patient nature. I was 13 when he died, and as he passed on, so did the wonders of childhood.

No Ifs, Ands, Or Butts; It's Time to Wake Up

What is she doing and why is she ignoring me? 'Puma' is asking herself as I doze on the couch. Frantically, she begins butting me in the head, nanny-goat style. I awaken to see her eyes open wide with terror and concern, although she calms down as I talk to her and pet her.

And then there is the time I arrived home from the city to find Jon fast asleep on my living room sofa, with 'Toy' feverishly butting her head into his. He is not responding. The look of alarm on her face is increasing. She glances at me nervously and frequently, as if she is extending a plea for help. Finally, I butt him in the head – with my hand. At last, a sign of life. Like 'Puma', 'Toy' is clearly relieved at the resurrection of her human companion.

Why head-butting? Maybe it's nature's gift to cats whose preoccupied owners wouldn't notice anything until they were hit over the head with it.

Scent Home From the Vet

Going to the vet can't be nearly as much fun as playing with a catnip mouse or chewing on a plant. So coming home from the vet should be a relief, right? Well, not always; at least in this house.

Upon its arrival home, the poor patient is hardly greeted lovingly by its fellow-felines. The moment that carrier is sprung, a chorus of hisses rises. Backs arch, teeth are bared and the poor victim retreats to the cabinet under the bathroom sink.

How cruel and heartless to ostracise this poor kitty who just underwent a traumatic ordeal. THEY didn't have to spend 20 minutes on a cold metal table being poked, prodded and contorted into myriad positions.

The others are baffled, meanwhile. WHO is that? A dog? We don't know that scent. It's unfamiliar; it's scaryAACK! Go away!

Fortunately, that Been-At-The-Vet scent dissipates shortly and the cat begins to take on her own recognisable one again. She is once again in good feline graces with the others as they plot together to shred the toilet paper.

Tripod Triumph

'Skynyrd' huddled in the corner of her cage, her nearly severed leg rendered useless. She became the victim of a fan-belt accident while seeking warmth under a car bonnet.

By order of my mother, she was set for euthanasia the following morning – but not if the vet had his way.

"She's a perfectly healthy cat", he explained. "She can adjust to her life comfortably with three legs. Why not consider amputation instead?"

So 'Skynyrd' was spared from her death sentence. And, indeed, she scarcely acknowledged the absence of her leg. In fact, she became increasingly agile, with graceful, effortless landings on only three legs. She even used the lack of her leg to her advantage, using her new streamlined size to wedge herself into previously unexplorable secret cat hiding spots.

While 'Skynyrd' accepted her fate, there were those who did not. And they were all human.

"Ew", they would proclaim disdainfully, upon seeing her. "That is so ugly. How could you love that?"

Well, when 'that' lost a leg, did she lose her charm? Was she less endearing and loveable? And would she ever love me less if I became 'ugly?'

Miss Cindy Circle

Perhaps one of the more quirky cat fetishes to observe was 'Cindy's' circle obsession. The 'circles', as they were nicknamed, are those elasticised terrycloth hair accessories used to secure pony-tails.

To 'Cindy', these simple fasteners were more fun than a nest of birds. At first, she would spend hours just batting a circle around; when she became bored with that, she would bring it back to my feet, where she would remain until I threw it for her retrieval.

How cute, your are thinking. Yes, for the first month or so, perhaps, until I noticed a rash of circle abductions from the counter of the bathroom sink.

No problem; I gave 'Cindy' her own personal circles and stowed a secret cache of my own in the medicine cabinet. She caught on to that ruse and learned to slide open the mirrored door to loot my private collection.

Meanwhile, these things were seemingly multiplying at an alarming rate. They were between the cushions on the couch, in the litter box, and floating in the water bowl.

Despite their over-abundance, 'Cindy' was

the only one allowed to have circles, by official declaration of 'Cindy', herself. If another cat seemed mildly entertained by one, 'Cindy' would promptly intervene and confiscate it.

This possessiveness was not limited to members of her species. She once tugged one from the end of my braid and had the nerve to glare at me accusingly.

'Cindy' is gone now, and with her, she took some of the sparkle she added to the world. But she did leave behind a legacy of circles. Once in awhile, I'll still come across a chewed and tattered circle and I have to smile – while wiping a stray tear from my cheek.

Conversing With 'Cairo' At 7 am

Ow, why are you hitting me? Can't you see I'm trying to wash my face? Get out of the sink. Good. Now stay out! Yes, I know you're pretty; now, leave! Let go, that's a blush brush, not a bird. Stop! Hey, don't rub against my arm. Now look what you made me do. I almost gouged my eye out with this mascara. Fine, I'll pet you. Nice, nice. Please get off the toilet seat lid. Sorry, I need to sit there more than you. Thank you. No, I said get down. You don't see me sitting in your litter box, do you?

AUTHOR'S NOTE: *The above anecdote was the last paragraph of Rosalie's wonderful letter to me, and I must compliment her on her warm, persuasive writing about her cats.*

Joan Bernstein, the noted feline therapist, relates her personal stories and triumphs:

Joe is a 74-year-old resident at a seniors' nursing home who never leaves his room. When the cats were scheduled to visit, he astonished the entire staff by joining the group in the activity room. Though he normally does not speak above a whisper, when asked if he would like to pet a cat, he responded audibly: "Yes!" He helped arrange his incapacitated left arm to support the cat on his lap, then stroked the cat with his right hand, responding to sensory and verbal stimuli with appropriate responses. He was willing to allow the cat to visit with other residents, but when the group was asked who would like to hold a cat again, he was the first to raise his hand. He remained even after the cats had been returned to their carriers, staying until the last resident had been helped from the room before he was willing to leave. He left smiling, with a souvenir cat show rosette pinned to his wheel-chair.

Linda is profoundly handicapped. During the first session scheduled for this day treatment centre, Linda, who is mentally-retarded and blind, maintained a fetal position on a floor mat. She responds so infrequently that no one is sure if she can be reached.

Linda does not use her hands, which are clenched to her chest. It took several attempts to bring an arm away from her body so that her hand could be placed on a cat. Repeatedly, her knuckles were rubbed against the cat's fur.

At first, I tried speaking softly, persuasively. No response. Then, more sharply, "Linda, open your hand. Open your hand so you can pet the cat. Open your hand." She opened her hand. Guiding her hand in a stroking motion, I said: "Keep petting the cat and she will purr." When I released her hand, she continued stroking, and 'Remy' began to purr.

I wanted to find out if Linda was simply imitating, or if she was connecting cognitive and motor responses, so I said, "Linda, 'Remy' loves to have her back scratched. Your hand is on 'Remy's' back." Without a pause, she curved her fingers slightly and shortened her strokes.

'Remy' purred louder. "The cat likes you, Linda. Do you like the cat?"

Linda's expressionless face tilted toward the sound of 'Remy's' purr and the physical vibration, and she grimaced. We later learned that this grimace is Linda's smile.

The cat had broken through years of barriers in 15 minutes, opening the way for Linda's therapists.

Linda now has a specially-constructed chair, contoured to her spinal curvature, which props her in a semi-upright position. On a recent visit, she 'saw' the cat's face with cupped hand, and with her fingertips, explored the cat's physical conformation. She attempted verbal identification. Each time the cat thrust her face into Linda's hand, Linda smiled.

ANSWERS TO I.Q. TEST

X - 1	Y - 6	I - 11	G - 16	F - 21
K - 2	P - 7	M - 12	V - 17	E - 22
C - 3	B - 8	H - 13	R - 18	Z - 23
L - 4	U - 9	O - 14	T - 19	D - 24
N - 5	S - 10	Q - 15	J - 20	A - 25
				W - 26

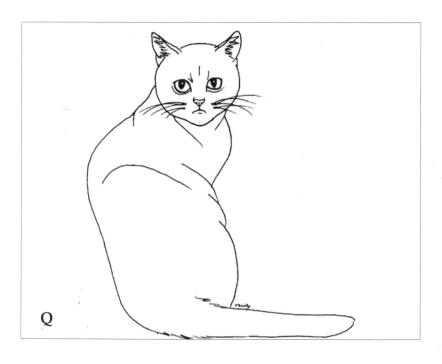

Q

Chapter X

Cat Language and Your Talking Cat

Most writers and professionals in other occupations find it useful to jot down or tape-record information which can be stored and retrieved at a later time.

You may want to adapt that same memory-jogging idea for gathering each day's Cat Language incidents as they occur. Let's say that your cat addressed you with some request that is momentarily confusing to you. You offer to let her out, for example, and she just sits there.

By process of elimination, you finally realise that her bowl of water is empty and her conversation focussed only on that. You fill the bowl and your cat looks up contentedly, saying, in effect, "I knew you'd eventually get the message. Thank you."

The keeping of a journal is more than just adding pictures to an album. If you can arrange to keep a camera handy, you can add a captioned memorandum to the picture of Tabby asking for water: 'Here she is asking for water. Notice how she raises her tail and swings the top of her tail to the left and right. Also, look at the way she holds out her tongue to indicate her thirst.'

Your journal can be organised in three columns as follows:

WHAT I SEE   WHAT I HEAR   WHAT IT SAYS

In Column One, mount the photos that demonstrate the body language which your cat is displaying. Try to match the eye, ear, tail and face messages in your photo with the examples in this book. Then, report as closely as possible the pitch, tone and volume of each phonetic sound your cat is expressing to accompany her body language.

If you can record an actual audio cassette of cat sounds – cross-related with each photograph – your journal will become a much more impressive project for yourself in review and for your cat-family friends when they visit. And while some books try to reproduce the technically accurate sounds on a computer-type page, 10 different writers might come up with 10 variations in spelling out the phonetics.

As one of the national soft-drink advertisers says, 'the real thing' makes any effort at putting cat sounds into people-spoken words or phrases a little ludicrous, don't you think? In this book, we've merely done our best to bring this problem into focus, with anatomically accurate sketches, created to look as true-to-life as possible. As you study each picture, using your imagination and play-backs of your own Talking Cat's vocalising, your mind can register 'silent sounds' for your ears to hear!

These 'hearing' illustrations, drawing upon all of the 19 known Cat Language basic sounds, do what we've seen no other book on cats do in this way. I think you'll agree.

You can read a hundred books on the subject of cats and not really get to *know* your cat, unless you are serious enough about wanting to communicate and *get involved*.

Just as people you know on the

Parent-Teachers Association give total lip-service to their membership and then fail to appear at the action meeting, or are never present when asked to join a committee, cat communications requires complete concentration and repeated follow through.

Why do 10 per cent of the students in any classroom excel in grades, while the other 90 per cent either 'just pass' or even fail? Any teacher will respond: *Getting involved.*

So, if you've ever kept an accurate diary, a nautical log, or a ledger, you're ready to enjoy a cat journal as never before.

In conjunction with the written aspects, don't forget to utilise the ultimate visual tool, *your camera.* Or, if you have a talent at pencil-sketching, better yet. Nothing makes a more lasting impression on the mind of a Cat Language learner than personal involvement with a good camera or a pencil and pad.

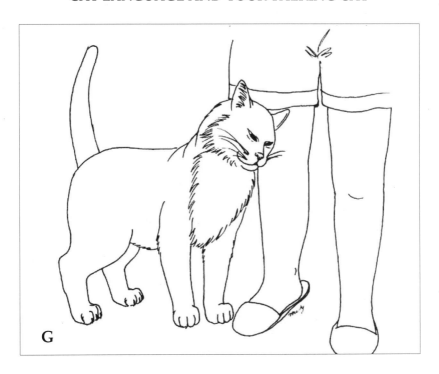

G

A. CAT BYE-LAWS

1. At any given time, the role of a cat-owner can, and will, be questioned, revoked or annulled by official whim of the cat itself.

2. All food is subject to approval. What works on Tuesday may fail miserably by Thursday.

3. Response to calling by owner is at the discretion of the cat, depending on its mood. After all, you don't always come running at the sound of your name, do you?

4. Used cotton swabs salvaged from the wastebasket are the plaything choice by 3-to-1 over designer mink toy mice.

5. Attention to cat must be paid immediately upon demand. Failure to do so will result in disruption of activity you are involved in at the time.

6. Litter boxes not meeting proper sanitary standards will be disregarded until conditions meet official cat approval.

7. New household additions (i.e., other felines and ESPECIALLY dogs!) must undergo a series of stringent preliminary tests before achieving full territorial acceptance status. Testing will vary among cats, but may include growling, hissing, snarling and swatting for the new arrival to endure over a period of one week to one month or more.

8. The cat may change its mind whenever it wishes and however many times it pleases. This also applies to reversing actions already in progress, especially in deciding to stay in after cajoling its sleeping owner to let it out.

B. CAT OWNER'S PLEDGE

I am the one who took over from your mother and am responsible for keeping you well and happy.

I will try to feed you well and protect you from the elements here in our nice home.

You are a member of our family and we love you.

You can come to me with any problem. If you need my help, you can have it.

Always tell me what's on your mind.

I sincerely want to understand you better.

I think you understand me because you are a very intelligent cat.

All I ask is that you love us as we love you.

Epilogue

I began with a Prologue and end with an Epilogue, in correct playwright style and in respectful deference to a little animal who has so much exciting theatre in its veins.

When you own a cat, you have a lifetime (for a cat, about 15 years) front-row-centre ticket to one of Mother Nature's most hypnotising spectacles.

And when you 'talk' with Your Talking Cat, you are joining an elite group of people who sense that communicating with a cat holds the promise of virtually endless hours of pure relaxation and amusement. More important, it is the key to obtaining the most pleasure and emotional satisfaction from your treasured companionship with your cat.

Busy as we all are, you now have some clues that will enable you to 'decode' a cat in seconds, where it may have taken you many minutes of puzzlement before.

Now that *Your Talking Cat* is winding down, I submit that the undeniable power of a cat's special language to communicate with us is one of the most challenging phenomenons which serious language students could address.

As we continue to open our minds, the cat will no longer sound like cat jabberwocky to us; she will not come across like a member of some alien race of anthropomorphic beings; rather, she will be accepted by us in her own right, as a species of a very highly emotional, very independent, yet very loving and very interesting little animal who would like to know us better, much better. And, if you want to find out something about yourself, just talk to a cat.

Like her, we are all one, on the same planet, spun out from the same errant star, more eons ago than our feeble minds can fathom. And even if Man, himself, does not appear capable of communicating with his own species without devastating wars, *wouldn't it be heartening to think that at least cats and people could succeed in living with each other and communicate in harmony?*

The Author

A POEM FOR MY TALKING CAT

Cut out and frame the little poem on the following page and set it near her sleeping place. Maybe she can't read it, but she KNOWS it says something nice about her. (Sign her name and yours on the blank lines underneath).

TO MY TALKING CAT

Cute as a button,
Full of fun and play,
How can I look at you
and not feel good today?

You lift my spirits
When I feel down.
You make me smile,
Erase my frown.

What, oh what
Would I ever do
Without so nice a friend as you?

That's why I'm reading
This book today.
To understand all the things you say.

_____   _____
    CAT   OWNER

Jack Richter has written on subjects as diverse as phobias and felines. His knowledge of language and communications, plus his insights into people and motivations, give YOUR TALKING CAT readers a refreshing change-of-pace. He lives in New York.

Other Books from Windsor